David Joe

How To Start Trading On Forex

A beginner's guide to forex trading

Copyright © 2022 by David Joe

All rights reserved. No part of this publication may be reproduced, stored or transmitted in any form or by any means, electronic, mechanical, photocopying, recording, scanning, or otherwise without written permission from the publisher. It is illegal to copy this book, post it to a website, or distribute it by any other means without permission.

David Joe asserts the moral right to be identified as the author of this work.

David Joe has no responsibility for the persistence or accuracy of URLs for external or third-party Internet Websites referred to in this publication and does not guarantee that any content on such Websites is, or will remain, accurate or appropriate.

Designations used by companies to distinguish their products are often claimed as trademarks. All brand names and product names used in this book and on its cover are trade names, service marks, trademarks and registered trademarks of their respective owners. The publishers and the book are not associated with any product or vendor mentioned in this book. None of the companies referenced within the book have endorsed the book.

First edition

This book was professionally typeset on Reedsy
Find out more at reedsy.com

Contents

Foreword 1
INTRODUCTION TO FOREX 2
What is traded on the Foreign exchange? 2
What is a Spot Market? 2
Which currencies are traded on Forex market? 2
When can currencies be traded? 2
WHY TRADE FOREIGN CURRENCIES 5
What devices Do i need To Start Trading Forex? 5
What Does It Cost To Trade Forex? 5
WHO TRADES FOREX? 8
1. Commercial & Investment Banks 8
2. Central Banks 8
3. Investment Managers and Hedge Funds 8
4. Multinational Corporations 8
5. Individual Investors 8
HOW YOU MAKE MONEY TRADING FOREX 10
How to Read an FX Quote 10
Can I still be able to trade if I don't have enough money to buy $10,000 euros? 10
TRADING SESSIONS 15
SESSION OVERLAP 15
Best Days Of The Week To Trade 15
When to Trade if you would like to Lose Money 15
Can't Trade During Busy Market Hours? 15
TYPES OF TRADERS 23
THE SIX DIFFERENT TYPES OF FOREX TRADER 23
1. Scalper 23
2. Day Trader 23
3. Swing Trader 23
4. Position Trader 23
5. Algorithmic Trader 23
6. Event- driven Trader 23
FOREX TERMINOLOGIES 26
WHAT IS A LOT IN FOREX? 35
BROKERS 39

What is a broker? What do they do? 39
TYPES OF BROKERS 39
FOREX VERSUS STOCKS 45
PROTECT YOURSELF BEFORE YOU WRECK YOURSELF........................47
TRADING PLATFORMS/INTERFACES 49
MT 4 AND MT 5 49
MONEY MANAGEMENT...53
Drawdown and Maximum Drawdown? 53
Don't Lose Your Shirt 53
Risk to Reward 53
Summary..53
WHY HAVE A TRADING PLAN? 60
Why Have a Trading Plan?..60
What Should be in Your Trading Plan? 60
ARE YOU WILLING TO PAY THE PRICE? 63
FOREX SCAMS 67

1.
2.
   1.
   2.
   3.
   4.
3.
   1.
   2.
4.
   1.
   2.
   3.
   4.
   5.
5.
   1.
   2.
6.

            1.
            2.
            3.
            4.
7.
    1.
            2.
            3.
            4.
            5.
            6.
            7.
8.
9.
10.
    1.
        2.
11.
12.
13.
    1.
14.
    1.
        2.
        3.
        4.
15.
    1.
        2.
16.

Foreword

The foreign exchange market "Forex" or "FX" as you may know it is a global marketplace for the trade off of currencies pairs priced in terms of one versus the other. Need I say this, the largest market all over the world is the Forex market.

What happens when I trade Forex? Forex trading can be puzzling especially for the noobies who are just or about to get in to the game. In this book "A beginners guide to Forex", contains all the vital knowledge you need to know about the Forex trading market before venturing into it and also majorly how to become a profitable and pro trader either as a beginner or even if you've already been trading the market.

INTRODUCTION TO FOREX

Forex ' FX ' refers to the market place where varied currencies and currency derivatives are traded, as well as to the currencies and currency derivatives traded there. Forex is the abstract from " Foreign exchange ". The Forex market is the largest, most liquid demand in the world by trading quantity, with trillions of dollars changing grasp every day. It has no central physical location, most of the trading is carried out through banks, brokers, and financial institutes.

Forex exists so that substantial amounts of one currency can be traded for the equal worth in another currency at the current market rate. Some of these trades come about because financial institutes, companies, or individualities who own a business needs to trade one currency for another. For instance, an American company may trade U.S. dollars for Japanese Yen in order to pay for goods that has been bought from Japan and is payable in Yen.

A large deal of Forex trade exists to hold speculation on the order of currency value. Traders gain from the price movement of a particular pair of currencies.

The Forex market is open 24 hours a day, five days a week, except for holidays or breaks. Although, the Forex market is open on numerous holidays or breaks on which stock markets are closed, in which the trading quantity may be minor.

What is traded on the Foreign exchange?

The plain response is money. Forex trading is the concurrent buying of one currency and the selling of another. Currencies are traded through a broker or dealer, and are traded in pairs; for instance the Euro dollar and the US dollar(EUR/ USD) or the British pound and the Japanese Yen(GBP/ JPY).

Because you're not purchasing anything physical, this type of trading can be confusing. Think of purchasing a currency as buying a share in a particular country. When you purchase, say, Japanese Yen, you are in outcome buying a share in the Japanese economy, as the price of the currency is a direct reflection of what the market thinks about the current and future wellness of the Japanese economy.

In general, the trade-off rate of a currency versus different currencies is a reflection of the order of that country's economy, compared to the different countries' economies.

Unlike other financial markets like the New York Stock Exchange, the Forex spot market has neither a physical place nor a central trade-off. The Forex market is considered an Over-the- Counter (OTC) or ' Interbank ' market, due to the reality that the entire market is runned electronically, within a network of banks, continuously over a 24- hour period.

Not until the late 1990's, only the " big guys " could venture this game. The foremost necessity existed that you could trade only if you had about ten to fifty million bucks to start with! Forex was originally intended to be used by bankers and big institutes and not by us " little guys ". In spite of that, because of the rise of the Internet, online Forex trading firms are currently able to offer trading accounts to 'retail' dealers like us.

All you need to get started is a computer/ smartphone, a high-speed Internet connection, and the information held within this book.

What is a Spot Market?

A spot market is any market that they deals in the current price of a monetary instrument.

Which currencies are traded on Forex market?

The most large currencies followed by their symbols are shown below.

Symbol	Country	Currency	Nickname
USD	United States	Dollar	Buck
EUR	Euro members	Euro	Fiber
JPY	Japan	Yen	Yen
GBP	Great Britain	Pound	Cable
CHF	Switzerland	Franc	Swissy
CAD	Canada	Dollar	Loonie
AUD	Australia	Dollar	Aussie
NZD	New Zealand	Dollar	Kiwi

Forex currency symbols are always three letters, where the first two letters distinguish the name of the country and the third letter identifies the name of that country's currency.

When can currencies be traded?

The spot FX market is special within the world markets. It's like a Super Walmart where the market is open 24- hours a day. At any time, nearly around the world a financial center is open for business, and banks and other institutes trade-off currencies every hour of the day and night with normally only minor breaks on the weekend.

The foreign exchange markets follow the sunlight around the world, therefore you can trade late at night(if you're a vampire) or in the morn(if you're an early bird). Keep in mind though, the early bird does not inescapably get the worm in this market you might get the worm but a bigger, nastier bird of prey can lurk up and consume you too.

Time Zone	New York	GMT
Tokyo Open	7:00 pm	0:00
Tokyo Close	4:00 am	9:00
London Open	3:00 am	8:00
London Close	12:00 pm	17:00
New York Open	8:00 am	13:00
New York Close	5:00 pm	22:00

WHY TRADE FOREIGN CURRENCIES

There are numerous benefits and advantages to trading Forex. Here are just some reasons why so many people are opting for this market.

- No commissions

No clearing charges, no trade- off charges, no government charges, no brokerage charges. Brokers are compensated for his or her services through commodity called the bid- ask spread.

- No intermediaries

Spot currency trading eliminates the middlemen, allowing you to trade or interact directly with the market responsible for the price of a particular currency pair.

- No fixed lot size

In the futures markets, lot or contract sizes are judged by the trades. An average- size deal of a silver futures is around 5000 ounces. In Forex, you can decide your own lot size. This allows traders to partake with accounts as small as $250(although I'll explain afterward why a $250 account is a poor ideal).

- Low deal costs

The retail deal cost(the bid— ask spread) is often times lower than 0.1 percent under usual market conditions. At great trades, the spread can be as low as 0.7 percent. In reality this depends on your leverage and all will be cleared subsequently.

- A 24- hour market

There is no waiting for the opening bell- from Sunday evening to Friday afternoon EST, the Forex market no way sleeps. This can be stupendous for those who want to trade on a part-time basis, because you'll be capable to opt when you need to trade — morning, noon or night.

- No one can control the market

The foreign exchange market is so huge and has so numerous partakers that no single individual(not even a central bank) can control the market price for an lengthy period of time.

- Leverage

In Forex trading, a small margin deposit can govern a greatly larger entire contract value. Leverage gives the trader the authority to make decent profits, and at the same time keep risk capital to a minimum. As an instance, Forex brokers give 200 to 1 leverage, which implies that a $50 dollar margin deposit would allow a trader to buy or sell $10,000 worth of currencies. Also, with $500 dollars, one could trade with $100,000 dollars and so on. But leverage could be a double-edged sword. Without proper risk management, this high degree of leverage can result in considerable losses as well as profit.

- High Liquidity

Because the Forex Market is so enormous, it's likewise extremely liquid. This implies that under normal market conditions, with a click of a mouse you'll be capable to promptly buy and sell at will. You are in no way " stucked " in any trade. You can also set your online trading platform to automatically close your position at your desired gain position(a limit order), and/ or close a trade if a trade is repositioning against you(a stopover loss setup).

- A Free " Demo " Accounts

You would suppose that getting started as a currency trader would cost a ton of money. The real fact is, likened to trading stocks, options or futures, it doesn't. Online Forex brokers offer " mini " and " micro " trading accounts, some with a minimal account deposit of $300 or lesser. Now I 'm not saying you should open an account with the bare minimum but it does makes Forex much more accessible to the average(poorer) individual who doesn't own a lot of start-up trading capital.

What devices Do i need To Start Trading Forex?

A computer/ smartphone with a high- speed Internet connection and all the information in this book is all that is required to begin trading currencies.

What Does It Cost To Trade Forex?

An online currency trading account may be opened for with a couple hundred bucks. Don't laugh – micro accounts and its bigger relative, the mini account, are both good ways to get your feet wet without drowning. For a micro account, I'd recommend at least $500 to $100,000 for a start. For a mini account, I'd recommend a minimum of $10,000 to begin.

WHO TRADES FOREX?

The Forex market not only has many players but many sorts of players. Here I list some of the major types of institutions and traders in Forex markets:

1. Commercial & Investment Banks

The largest volume of currency is traded in the inter bank market. This is often where banks of all sizes trade currency with each other and through electronic networks. Big banks counts for a big percentage of total currency volume trades. Banks aid Forex transactions for clients and carry out speculative trades from their own trading desks.

2. Central Banks

Central banks, which represent a nation's government, are extremely important players within the Forex market. Open market operations and rate of interest policies of central banks influence currency rates to a very large extent.

A central bank is liable for fixing the price of its local currency on Forex. This is often the exchange rate regime by which its currency will trade in the open market. Rate of exchange regimes are divided into floating, fixed and pegged types. Any action taken by a central bank in the Forex market is done to limit fluctuation or increase the competitiveness of that nation's economy.

3. Investment Managers and Hedge Funds

Portfolio managers, pooled funds and hedge funds structure the second-biggest collection of players in the Forex market next to banks and central banks. Investment managers trade off currencies for giant accounts such as pension funds, foundations, and endowments.

An investment manager with a global portfolio will have to purchase and sell currencies to trade foreign securities.

4. Multinational Corporations

Firms engaged in importing and exporting. They conduct Forex transactions to pay money for goods and services. Consider the case of a German solar panel producer that imports American components and sells its finished products in China. After the ultimate sale is made, the Chinese yuan the producer received must be converted back to euros. The German firm must then exchange euros for dollars to get more American components.

5. Individual Investors

The amount of Forex trades made by retail investors is extremely low compared to financial institutions and companies. However, it is growing rapidly in popularity. Retail investors base currency trades on a combination of fundamentals (i.e., rate of interest parity, inflation rates, and monetary policy expectations) and technical factors (i.e., support, resistance, technical indicators, price patterns).

HOW YOU MAKE MONEY TRADING FOREX

In the FX market, you either purchase or sell currencies. Placing a trade on the foreign exchange market is simple: the mechanics of a trade are very similar to those found in other markets (like the stock market), so if you've got any experience in trading, you ought to be able to pick it up pretty quickly.

The purpose of Forex trading is to exchange one currency for another with the expectation that the price will change, so that the currency you bought will increase in value compared to the one you sold.

Example of making money by buying Euros

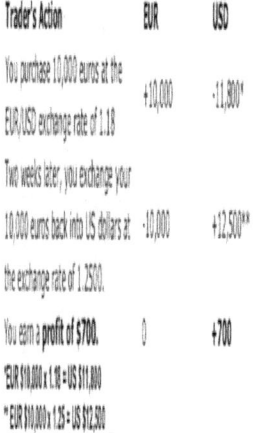

Trader's Action	EUR	USD
You purchase 10,000 euros at the EUR/USD exchange rate of 1.18	+10,000	-11,800*
Two weeks later, you exchange your 10,000 euros back into US dollars at the exchange rate of 1.2500.	-10,000	+12,500**
You earn a **profit of $700**.	0	+700

*EUR 10,000 x 1.18 = US $11,800
**EUR 10,000 x 1.25 = US $12,500

A rate of exchange is solely the rate of one currency estimated against another currency. For instance, the USD/ CHF rate of exchange indicates how many U.S. dollars can purchase one Swiss franc, or what percentage of Swiss francs you need to purchase one U.S. dollar.

How to Read an FX Quote

Currencies are forever quoted in pairs, like GBP/ USD or USD/ JPY. The main reason they're quoted in pairs is because in every foreign exchange transaction you're simultaneously purchasing one currency and selling another. Below is an example of a foreign rate of exchange for the British pound versus the U.S. dollar

GBP/ USD = 1.7500

The first listed currency to the left of the slash(/) is known as the base currency(in this sample, the British pound), while the other on the right is called the counter or quote currency(in this case, the U.S. dollar).

When purchasing, the exchange rate tells you how much you have to pay in units of the quote currency to buy one unit of the base currency. Within the sample above, you've got to pay 1.7500 U.S. dollar to buy 1 British pound.

When selling, the rate of exchange tells you how many units of the quote currency you will get for selling one unit of the base currency. Within the illustration over, you will receive 1.7500 U.S. dollars once you sell 1 British pound.

Long/ Short

First, you ought to determine whether you need to buy or sell.

However, if you suppose the base currency will rise in value and also sell it back at a higher price, then you would want to buy(which really means purchasing the base currency and selling the quote currency). In trader's term, this is often called " going long " or taking a " long position ". Just remember long = buy.

Likewise, if you suppose the base currency would fall in value and then purchasing back at a lower price, then you would like to sell(which actually means selling the base currency and buying the quote currency). Also in trader's term is often called " going short " or " taking a short position ".

Bid— Ask Spread

All Forex quotes involve a two- way price, the bid and ask. The bid price is often lesser than the ask price.

The bid price is the price in which the dealer is ready to purchase the base currency in exchange for the quote currency. This implies the bid is the price at which you (as the trader) will sell.

The ask price is the price in which the dealer will sell the base currency in exchange for the quote currency. This implies the ask is the price at which you'll buy.

The contrast between the bid and also the ask price is popularly known as the spread.

Let's take a glance at an illustration of a price quote taken from a trading platform:

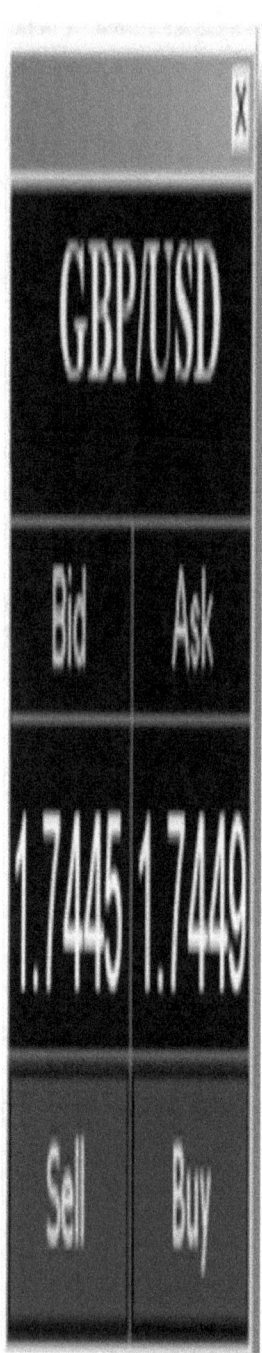

On this GBP/ USD quote, the bid price is 1.7445 and the ask price is 1.7449. That's how brokers makes it so freely for you to trade off your money.

However, you click" Sell" and you'll sell If you want to sell GBP at 1.7445. Or, you click" Buy" If you want to buy GBP at 1.7449.

In the following cases, we are going to use fundamental analysis to help us determine whether to buy or sell a specific currency pair.

- EUR/ USD

In this case Euro is the base currency and therefore the " basis " for the buy/ sell.

If you believe that the US economy will continue to weaken, you would carry out a BUY EUR/ USD order. By doing so you have purchased Euros in the anticipation that they will rise versus the US dollar.

If you suppose that the US economy is strong and the euro will weaken against the US dollar you would carry out a SELL EUR/ USD order. By doing so you have sold Euros in the anticipation that they will fall versus the US dollar.

- USD/ JPY

In this case the US dollar is the base currency and therefore the " base " for the buy/ sell.

If you suppose that the Japanese government is going to weaken the Yen in order to assist its exporting industry, you would carry out a BUY USD/ JPY order. By doing so you have bought U.S dollars in the anticipation that they will rise versus the Japanese yen.

If you think that Japanese investors are pulling money out from the U.S. financial markets and converting all their U.S. dollars back to the Japanese Yen, as this will hurt the US dollar, you would carry out a SELL USD/ JPY order. By doing so you have sold U.S dollars in the anticipation that they will devaluate against the Japanese yen.

- GBP/ USD

In this study the GBP is the base currency and therefore the " base " for the buy/ sell.

If you suppose the British economy will continue to do better than the United States in terms of economic growth, you would also carry out a BUY GBP/ USD order. By doing so you have bought pounds in the anticipation that they will rise versus the US dollar.

If you believe the British's economy is retarding while the United State's economy stays strong like a bull, you would carry out a SELL GBP/ USD order. By doing so you have sold pounds in the anticipation that they will devaluate against the US dollar

- USD/ CHF

In this case the USD is the base currency and therefore the " base " for the buy/ sell.

However, you would carry out a BUY USD/ CHF if you suppose the Swiss franc is depreciating . By doing so you have bought US dollars in the anticipation that they will appreciate versus the Swiss Franc.

Same goes otherwise, you would execute a SELL USD/ CHF order, If you believe that the US housing market bubble burst will hurt future economic growth. By doing so you have sold US dollars in the anticipation that they will depreciate against the Swiss franc.

Can I still be able to trade if I don't have enough money to buy $10,000 euros?

You'll be able to with margin trading! Margin trading is simply the term used for trading with borrowed capital. This can be how you're able to open $10,000 or $100,000 positions with as little as $50 or $1,000. You'll be able to conduct relatively large transactions, very quickly and cheaply, with a small amount of initial capital.

Margin trading within the foreign exchange market is quantified in "lots". For now, just consider the term "lot" as the minimum amount of currency you have to buy. When you go to the grocery store and want to buy an egg, you can't just buy one egg; they come in dozens or "lots" of 12. In Forex, it might be just as foolish to buy or sell $1 EUR, So therefore they usually come in "lots" of $10,000 or $100,000 depending on the type of account you have.

TRADING SESSIONS

Now that you know what Forex is, why you must trade it, and who makes up the Forex market, it's about time you learned when you can trade. You can make money trading when the market moves up, and you'll even make money when the market moves down. **BUT** you may have a very difficult time trying to make money when the market doesn't move at all. And believe it, there'll be times when the market is as still as the victims of Medusa.

This chapter will help determine when the most effective times of the day are to trade. Before observing the best times to trade, we must take a look at what a 24-hour day in the Forex world looks like. The Forex market are often broken up into four major trading sessions: the Sydney session, the Tokyo session, the London session, and Trump's favorite time to tweet (before he was banned), the New York session.

Historically, the Forex market has three peak trading sessions. Traders often specialise in one of the three trading periods, instead of attempt to trade the markets 24 hours per day.

This is known as the "Forex 3-session system". These sessions comprises the Asian, European, and North American sessions, which also are called Tokyo, London, and New York sessions. Some traders opt to differentiate sessions by names of the continent, other traders choose to use the names of the cities.

SESSION OVERLAP

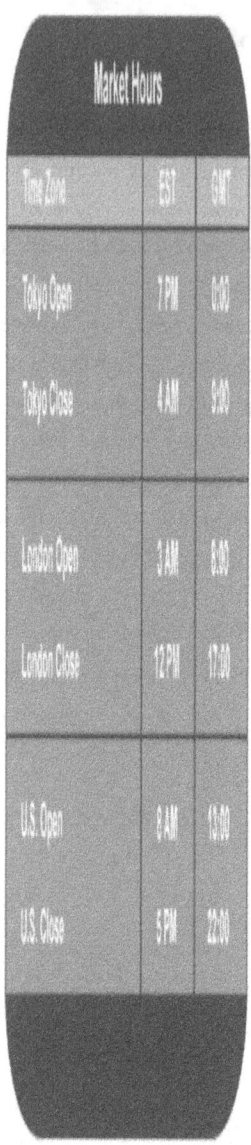

Also notice that in between each Forex trading session, there's a period of time where two sessions are open at the same time.

For example, during the summer from 3:00-4:00 AM ET, the Tokyo session and London session overlap. and during both summer and winter from 8:00 AM-12:00 PM ET, the London session and also the New York session overlap.

Naturally, these are the busiest times during the trading day because there's more volume when two markets are open at the same time. This is sensible because during those times, all the market participants are wheelin' and dealin', which implies that more money is transferring hands.

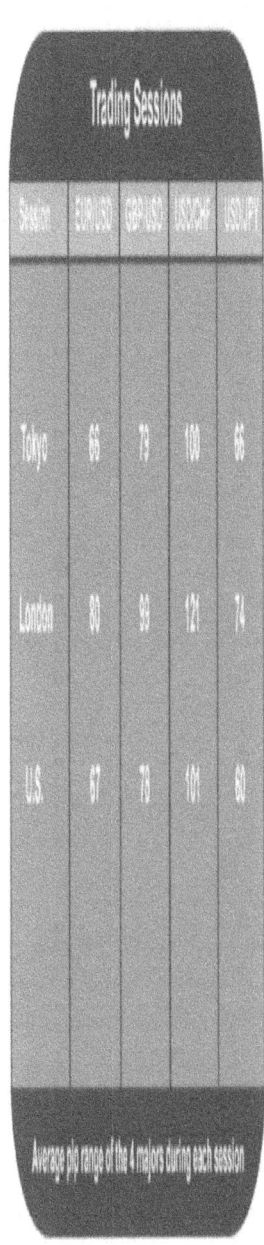

As you can see, the London session usually shows the most movement.

Now let's take a look at which days of the week are best for trading.

Best Days Of The Week To Trade

So now that we know the London session is the busiest out of all the other sessions, but there are also certain days in the week where all the markets tend to show more movement. Below is a chart of average pip range for the 4 major currency pairs for each day of the week;

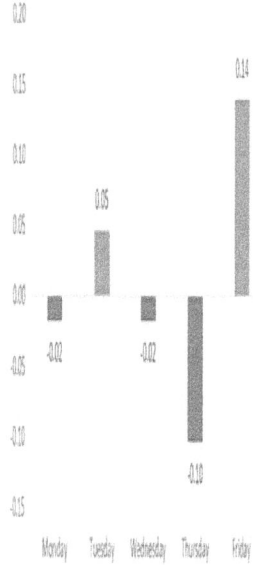

Best Day of the Week to Trade

As we can see that during the middle of the week is where the most movement is seen on all 4 major pairs. Fridays are usually busy until 12pm EST when the market pretty much drops dead until it closes at 5pm EST. This simply means we only work half-days on Fridays. The weekend always starts early! Yippee!

So based on these three basic pieces, we have gotten the knowledge of when the busiest times of the market are. These are the most effective times to trade because they give us a higher chance of success.

If you're feeling down in the dumps and wish to lose money, these are the days to trade…

When to Trade if you would like to Lose Money

I wouldn't like to force my opinions on you. Instead, I want you to make your own decisions when it comes to your own trading. If you actually do not want to trade during the busier times of the market when trade volume and pip movement is highest and where you will make money easier, then by all means, be at liberty to trade on these times mentioned below. I guarantee you'll have a harder time trading!

Fridays: Fridays are very unpredictable. This is often a good day to trade if you want to lose all the profit you made during the rest of the week.

Sundays: There's very little movement on these days. Trade on this day if you want to begin your week with **NEGATIVE** pips.

Holidays: Banks are closed which simply means very little amount for whatever country is having the holiday. Holidays are great to trade once you would rather lose your money than take a day off and enjoy the other finer things in life.

News Reports: Nobody really knows where the price will go when a news report comes out. You may lose a fortune trading during news releases if you don't know what you're doing. Price acts like a sort of drunken monkey during these times and become unpredictable.

Can't Trade During Busy Market Hours?

What you can do if you can't trade during the busy market hours.

If you reside in a crappy time zone or you have a day job, then you almost certainly can't sit in front of a computer during the busy market hours. If this describes you, then I've got a few solutions for you:

- Move to a much better time zone:

Move to London preferably. Sure you'd need to pack up and start a whole new life, but hey, at least you can trade right? Trade at work (be sure you have some "real" work available just in case your boss sneaks up behind you and ask you what you're working on). I also recommend you master the ALT-TAB key combination (if you make use of Windows) so you can quickly switch windows at a moment's notice. This option can be the last perk because your employer is mainly paying you while you trade Forex. Gettin' paid while gettin' paid if you get what I'm sayin'.

- Become a swing or position trader:

As a swing/position trader, you won't need to constantly monitor the markets and you can check or look at them when you get off work.

- Trade a special session even if it's not the busiest one:

If you can't trade the London or U.S. session, then trade the Tokyo session. However, you must be disciplined and trade it every day. You'll start to learn how it moves and can develop strategies that are specific to that session.

I believe 2 and 3 are your best options, but again, the decision is up to you.

Even if you can't trade, it's good to observe the charts for a full session. By getting use to seeing the price movement in action, you'll be able to actually see the real story of the currency. Watching the charts live is extremely different than looking at past charts.

Even if you can't actually trade the market, take notes of when you would make trades while you're watching the charts live. Practice makes perfect, and therefore the more you do it, the better you'll get at it. **The choice Is Yours**

There you've got it! I've given you all the information you need regarding when the best times to trade are. All you've got to do now is decide whether or not you would rather trade when it's easier to make money, or if you'd rather have a go at it the hard way.

Summary

Busiest/Best times to trade:

- When there are 2 sessions overlapping: 3-4am EST and 8am-12pm EsT

The London session is still the most busiest out of the other two.

The mid— week typically shows the most movement.

Worst times to trade:

- Fridays
- Sundays
- Holidays
- News Events:During Desperate Housewives or American Idol episodes.

TYPES OF TRADERS

There are many types of Forex traders, and each demands a different approach. Whether you decide on the fast-paced sprint of day trading or the prolonged marathon of position trading, selecting the right style for you will maximize your chance of success.

THE SIX DIFFERENT TYPES OF FOREX TRADER

Forex traders tend to suit into one of the following six trading types: *scalper, day trader, swing trader, position trader, algorithmic trader, and event-driven trader*. Go through the separate types of traders below and discover the character that are optimal for each.

1. Scalper

Scalpers are short-term traders centered on holding positions for time frames as short as a few seconds to a few minutes. Forex scalping strategies involve trading constantly throughout the day, with the purpose of achieving small gains at the busiest (most liquid) times.

2. Day Trader

Day traders also execute frequent trades on an intraday time-frame . While their routine won't be as fast paced as a scalper's, day traders will similarly close all positions before the end of the trading day, so as not to hold any overnight. This implies trades are not affected by negative news that can hit prices before the market opens or after it closes.

To be successful as a day trader, you'll have to be ready to adapt to quick changes in price, as well as be cognizant of techniques important to this style of trading, such as fading the gap.

3. Swing Trader

Swing traders remain onto trades for longer than a single day, and up to perhaps a couple of weeks. Over this short time-frame , swing traders will typically favor technical analysis over fundamentals, although they ought to still be attuned to the news events that can trigger volatility.

4. Position Trader

Position traders keep up trades for an extended periods of time, from several weeks to years. As the longest holding period among trading styles, position traders are less inquisitive about an asset's short-term price fluctuations and more concerned, naturally, with the performance over more sustained time frames.

As a Forex position trader, you'll require patience as your money will often be locked up for a long time of periods. Particularly with long term trades, an intensive knowledge of fundamental factors is beneficial, so advanced analytical skills will serve you well.

5. Algorithmic Trader

Algorithmic traders depend on computer programs to set up trades for them at the best possible prices. Traders can apply defined instructions, or to either code the programs themselves, or purchase existing products.

6. Event- driven Trader

Event- driven traders make use of fundamental analysis to technical charts to inform their decisions. They'll seek to profit from spikes caused by political or economic events, similar as Non-Farm Payroll data, GDP, employment figures, and elections.

This type of trading will suit a person who likes to keep up with world news, and who'll understand how events can influence markets. Inquisitive, curious and forward thinking, you'll be proficient at processing new information and predicting how global and localized events may play out.

FOREX TERMINOLOGIES

1. Currency

The world's currencies are traded on the Foreign exchange market. The United Nations presently recognize 180 currencies that are used in 195 countries across the world. Some samples of currencies are the US dollar, the Euro, the British pound and the Japanese yen, which all act as a store of value and which are traded on Forex.

2. Currency pair

Although currencies are traded on the Forex market, we're not able to buy or sell single currencies. Whenever we place a trade in the market, we have to trade on currency pairs. Currency pairs comprises two currencies – the first one is the base currency and the second one the counter-currency or the quote currency.

3. Major pairs

In general, currency pairs are frequently grouped into major pairs, cross pair, and exotic pairs. Major pairs are pairs of currency that include the US dollar as either the base currency or counter-currency and one of the other seven major currencies (EUR, CAD, GBP, CHF, JPY, AUD, NZD).

If you're just beginning with trading, you ought to concentrate on the Major pairs since they generally offer truly low transaction costs and enough liquidity to avoid high slippage. Samples of major pairs are EUR/ USD, GBP/ USD and USD/ CHF.

4. Cross pairs and exotics pairs

Cross pairs, on the contrary hand include any two major currencies except the US dollar. Unlike major pairs, cross pairs have higher transaction costs and at times of lower liquidity, dealers can face slippage. Cross pairs also are usually more unpredictable than major pairs. Examples of the cross pairs include EUR/ GBP, EUR/ CHF and AUD/ NZD.

Finally, exotic pairs include exotic currencies which are not in the Top 10 of the most traded currencies, like the Mexican peso, Turkish lira or Czech koruna. Since those currencies are often extremely unpredictable, they ought to be left to be traded by the pros.

5. Exchange rate

The rate of exchange of a currency pair is what all traders follow. The rate of exchange is often simply called the price, since it shows the price of the base currency expressed in terms of the counter-currency. For instance, if the rate of exchange of EUR/ USD is 1.15, this suggests that one euro costs $1.15, or it takes $1.15 US dollar to buy one euro.

An increment in the exchange rate of a currency pair shows that the base currency is appreciating against the counter-currency or that the counter-currency is depreciating against the base currency. Also, a fall in the exchange rate shows that the base currency is devaluating against the counter-currency or that the counter-currency is appreciating against the base currency.

6. Bid Ask price

In any given moment, each currency pair has two exchange rates or prices – the bid price and the ask price. **What's the difference between those two?** The bid price is the price in which a buyer is willing to buy, while the ask price is the price in which sellers are willing to sell.

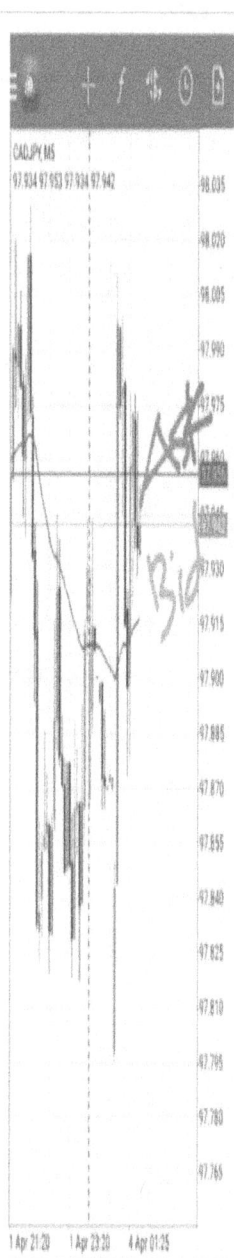

Presented its nature, the bid price is always lesser than the ask price. Once the two prices meet, either when the seller lower their ask price to meet a buyer's bid price or when the buyer increase their rate they're willing to pay for a currency and catch on a seller's ask price, a transaction occurs.

At the end, the buyer buy at the ask price, and the seller sell at the bid price. This simply implies that each price plotted on your chart is a representation of the market equilibrium at that point of time – the price at which the majority of market participants are willing to make a transaction.

7. Spread

Whenever you enter into a trade, you've got to pay transaction costs for that trade. While most brokers don't charge for commissions and fees on placing trades nowadays, the bid/ask spread remains the main cost to Forex traders. When buyer's buy at the ask price (the price at which sellers are willing to sell), their position is instantly in a loss that equals the bid/ask spread.

If you're a day trader or scalper, you would like to pay attention to the bid/ask spread since it can eat a large portion of your profits at the end of the day. Swing traders and position traders who have a longer-term approach to trading are less suffering from the spread as they open a smaller number of positions and have relatively higher profit targets.

8. Pip

When Forex traders discuss profits or losses, they typically use the term "pips". A pip is the short form of Percentage in Point and represents the smallest increment that an exchange rate can move up or down. Usually, one pip is equal to the fourth decimal of most currency pairs.

For instance, if EUR/USD is currently trading at 1.1558 and increased to 1.1562, that rise would equal to a change of 4 pips. However, some currency pairs have their pips located at the second decimal place, mostly the yen-pairs. If USD/JPY currently trades at 110.25 and falls to 110.10, that fall would be equal to a change of 15 pips.

While for gold(XAU/USD), the pips is found at the first decimal place.

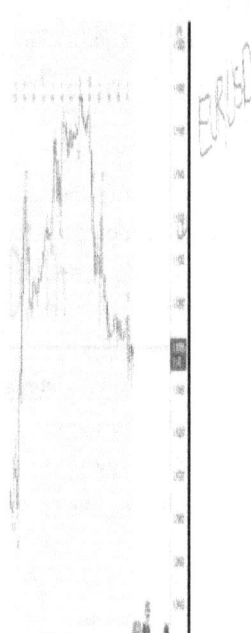

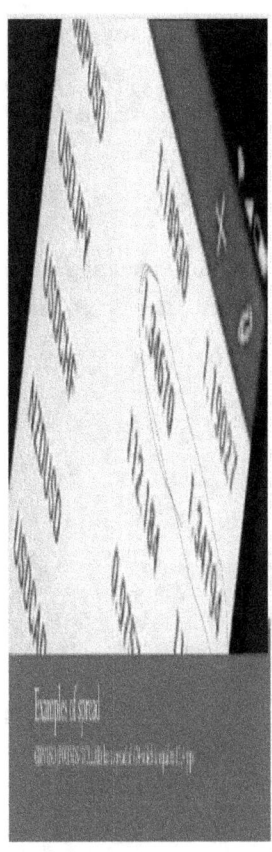

Example of spread
(EUR/USD 2.1 pips, or 2 pips and 1 pipette)

9. Pipette

A pip represents the fourth decimal place of most currency pairs, but there is even a smaller increment that prices can change.

It is called a pipette and it equals to 1/10 of a pip, i.e. 10 pipettes are one pip. A pipette is found at the fifth decimal place of most currency pairs (while in the yen-pairs, they're at the third decimal place).

Most traders usually don't follow movements in pipettes, even though some brokers use them in their trading platform. Today, pipettes are now mostly used as yardstick to measure the bid/ask spread, where a tenth of a pip is needed. For instance, the spread in a EUR/USD might be 1.4 pips or a pip and four pipettes.

10. Going long/short

This shouldn't be new to you anymore. Going long simply means to buy /purchase a currency pairs, while going short means to sell a currency pairs.

11. Support

A support level is a previous low in which the price has a big chance to retrace and move up.

Support and resistance are one of the most important and vital concepts in technical analysis. Technical traders analyze price moves only as they believe that the price reflects are available.

12. Resistance

Just like the support levels, resistance levels are also a vital tool in a technical trader's toolbox. While the support levels are based on previous lows, resistance levels track previous highs at which the price had difficulties to break above.

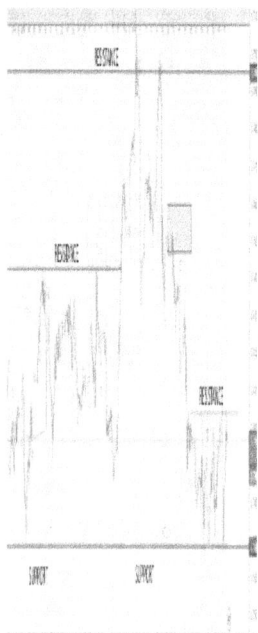

13. Leverage

The Forex market is available around the clock and offers traders to profit not just on rising prices, but also on falling ones. However, there is another reason to why a large number of traders gets attracted to the Forex market–leverage.

Trading on leverage allows traders to open a bigger size position than their initial trading account size would otherwise allow, and the Forex market is also known for extremely high leverage ratios offered by retail brokers.

For example; A 100:1 leverage allows a trader to open a position that is a hundred time larger than their initial deposit. If you deposit a minimum of $1,000, you're allowed to open a position size that's equal to $100,000!

However, do bear in mind that trading on an extremely high leverage is very risky, as it boosts not only your profits, but also your losses. Beginners should consider trading on a lower leverage until they get enough experience and screen time. This will help reduce losses and make sure that you stay in the game on the long run.

14. Margin

When also trading on leverage, your broker will allocate a portion of your trading account size as the collateral for the leveraged trade. This collateral is called "Margin" and its size depends totally on the leverage ratio that you're trading on. A leverage ratio of 100:1 requires for a margin that is equal to 1% of your position size.

Example; If you open a $100.000 position size using a 100:1 leverage, your margin will equal $1,000, which is 1% of the position size. Similarly if you open a position size of $40

NOTE!!! What's significant when dealing on leverage is to constantly observe an eye on your free margin. Your free margin equals your whole equity(account size any unrealized profits losses), minus your used margin. However, you 'll take a margin call and all your open trades will be made at the current market rate.

15. Lot size

The position size you carry on the market determines the size of your profits and losses in dollar value by affecting the value of one pip. In Forex market, a standard lot(standard position size) is equal to 100.000 units of the base currency. For instance, if you take one standard lot in the EUR/ USD pair, you're actually trading 100,000 euros with a pip- value equal to $10.

Fortunately, traders with lesser account sizes can take lower trades with mini-lots(10.000 units of the base currency) and micro-lots(1.000 units of the base currency.) Some brokers truly allow you to trade on a nano- lots(100 units of the base currency). In any of the cases, calculate your lot size in dependence of the size of your stop- loss so that you can remain inside your risk- management boundaries.

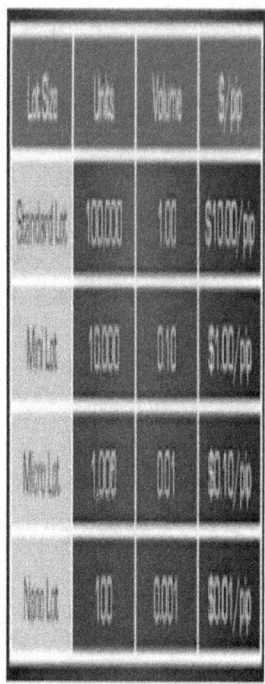

16. Bulls

The buyers are referred to as bulls.

17. Bears

The sellers are referred to as bears.

18. Ranging/ Trending

A market is considered ranging if it does not have any particular direction. It is neither moving upward or downward.

WHILE, a market is considered Trending when it has a direction. It is either moving upward or downward.

19. Bullish/Bearish Market

A market is said to be bullish when it's going upward.

WHILE, a market is bearish when it's going downward.

WHAT IS A LOT IN FOREX?

Forex is commonly traded in specific amounts called lots, or basically the number of currency units you will buy or sell.

A "lot" is a unit used in measuring a transaction amount. When you place an order on your trading platform, the orders are placed in sizes quoted in lots.

It's just like an egg carton (or an egg box in British English). When you want to buy eggs, you usually buy a carton (or box) of it. One carton contains 12 eggs.

The standard size of a lot is 100,000 units of currency, and now we also have the mini, micro, and nano lot sizes that are 10,000, 1,000, and 100 units respectively.

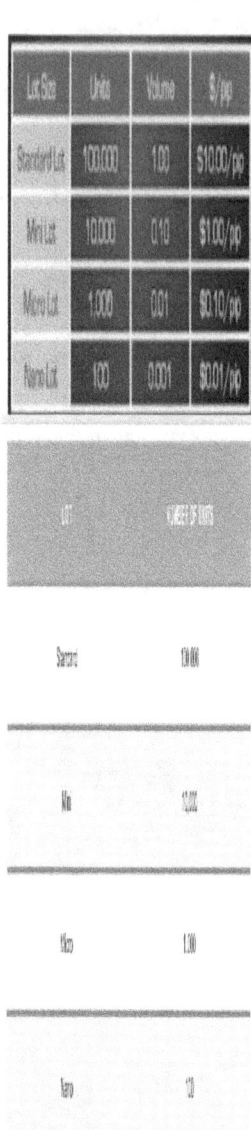

Some brokers do show their quantity in "lots", while other brokers show the actual currency units.

As you already know, the change in a currency value relative to another currency value is measured in "pips," which is a very very small percentage of a unit of currency's value.

To have an upper hand of this minute change in value, you need to trade large amounts of a particular currency in order to see any significant profit or loss.

Let's assume we are going to be using a 100,000 unit (standard) lot size. Let us now recalculate some examples to see how it affects the pip value.

USD/JPY at an exchange rate of 119.70: (.01 / 119.80) x 100,000 = $8.35 per pip

USD/CHF at an exchange rate of 1.4555: (.0001 / 1.4888) x 100,000 = $6.72 per pip

In some cases where the U.S. dollar is not quoted as the first in the currency pairs, the formula is slightly different.

EUR/USD at an exchange rate of 1.1940: (.0001 / 1.1940) X 100,000 = 8.38 x 1.1940 = $10 per pip

GBP/USD at an exchange rate of 1.8090: (.0001 / 1.8090) x 100,000 = 5.53 x 1.8090 = $10 per pip.

Below are some examples of pip values for EUR/USD and USD/JPY, depending on their lot size.

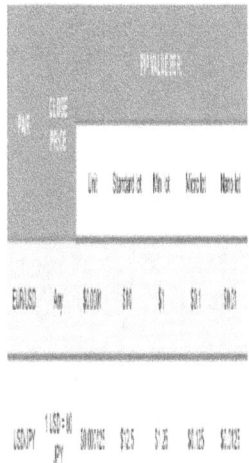

Your broker may have a different way for calculating pip values in respect to lot size but whatever way they do it, they'll should be able to tell you what the pip value is for the currency you are trading at the particular time.

So in other words, they do all the mathematics calculation for you!

As the market moves, so also will the pip value depending on the currency you are trading currently.

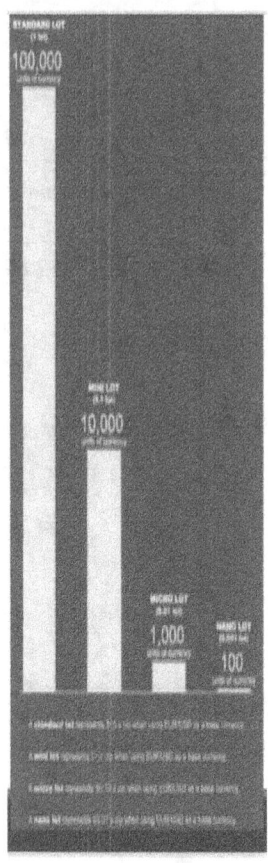

BROKERS

What is a broker? What do they do?

A broker is a person who buys and sells things on behalf of other people. A broker may also arrange transactions between a purchaser and vendor. After the parties have completed the deal, one of them pays the broker a commission.

When brokers also act as purchasers or sellers, they become the principal party to the deal.

A broker may be a firm. The firm acts as an agent for a customer, who pays it a commission for its services.

A Forex broker is a financial services company that provides traders access to a platform for buying and selling foreign currencies. Transactions in the Forex market are always between a pair of two different currencies. A Forex broker may also known be as a retail Forex broker or a currency trading broker.

TYPES OF BROKERS

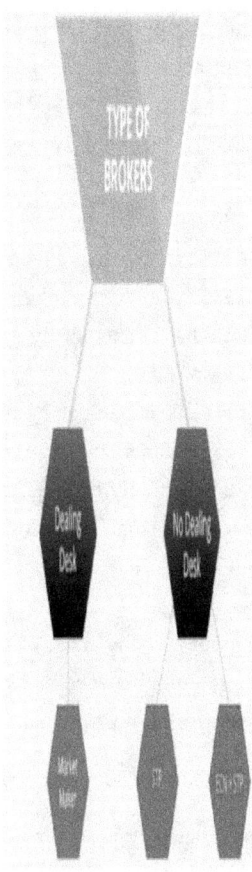

To deal or not to deal?

The first thing that should come across your mind when looking for a Forex Broker is whether or not they have a "dealing desk".

The term dealing desk takes root from a good old fashioned offline trading, when financial institutions actually do have a desk where the traders would sit and manage the institution's investments. Nowadays a "dealing desk" would more likely be a room filled with dozens if not hundreds of traders and analysts.

In a brokerage firm, a dealing desk refers to a team of traders who manage the broker's inventory and also the hedging operations.

Brokers that work with a dealing desk run their operations in a closed environment in which they set their own price rates and fill their clients orders either by matching the buy and sell orders of their clients, or by taking the counter party of the order if it can't be matched. When a broker has a dealing desk they call them a Market Maker.

Brokers that don't have a dealing desk do get their price quotes from the interbank market and make their orders by linking them directly to liquidity providers such as banks, hedge funds, mutual funds, or other brokers. If a broker doesn't have a dealing desk they are either an ECN (Electronic Communication Network) broker or an STP (Straight Through Processing) broker.

Market Makers

Forex Brokers that are "Market Makers" literally produce a market for their clients, meaning that all Forex deals are conducted internally out of an inventory, either by looking for a match for each deal out of the pool of orders coming in from other clients, or by the broker taking the counterparty themselves.

Because Market Makers don't take the deals out into the inter bank market, they are able to set their own prices. There is a common misconception amongst traders that Market Makers are mainly betting against their clients success. However, this is purely not true, as these Forex brokers will quote both a buy and a sell price that move together. Therefore, most of the profits or gains made by these Forex brokers come from spreads.

Electronic Communications Network (ECN) Broker

A true ECN broker connects traders directly with counter parties in the inter bank market. The only part the broker plays in the transaction is creating the link between buyers and sellers. They do not set their own price rates or manage inventories in any way, as all the price rates are taken directly from the inter bank market.

Straight Through Processing (STP) Brokers

Like true ECN brokers, STP brokers don't have a dealing desk, but they hire some of the practices of Market Maker brokers in order to provide more flexible trading conditions to their client and bypass some of the limitations of trading exclusively within the inter bank market.

ROLES OF FOREX BROKERS

The foreign exchange market is the largest global non-centralized exchange where trading process performed electronically via networks. The primary Forex participants are international banks and financial institutions operating huge volumes through a need to exchange currencies, presented as currency pairs, and assisting international business with the conversion which is known as the inter bank market.

While the major role of the Forex brokers is to provide access to trade Forex Markets or other Instruments mostly to the retail traders, allowing them to start with small investments and allowing access to trading to almost every individual interested in Forex Trading.

REGULATED FOREX BROKER

Forex being a decentralized market and increasing establishment of Forex brokers, pushed various world countries, established particular organizations or authorities in order to control the market proposals and regulate Forex Broker firms. So YES, Forex brokers are regulated while holding a license from a local authority similarly world-known FCA in the UK, ASIC in Australia, Commodity Futures Trading Commission CFTC in the USA, MAS in Singapore and lot more.

In extension to its constant check on the service providing, authorities protecting clients through compensation schemes and other security checks, allowing traders to fill the complaint which outcome may affect in heavy company fining or even dismiss. However, these conditions and regulating may differ from the regulator to another.

Making it simple, regulated broker means that you will trade Forex with proper security of funds and investment itself, supervising of the broker so first of all good broker is a sharply regulated broker.

WHAT MAKES A GREAT BROKER?

The Forex broker should be regulated since the Forex market is decentralized. What makes Brokers a great broker is its reliability and trust, which is provided by regulations. Obviously, this is the biggest trump you may trip as a retail trader if you choose a non-reliable, mainly non-regulated or offshore firm without a proper license you may easily fall into a scam and lose your money.

HOW TO CHOOSE BEST FOREX BROKER?

Security of funds is always first in Forex trading. For this reason, we recall your attention to opening an account with Regulated Brokers only.

Choose sharply regulated broker with top-tier license like FCA, ASIC, CFTC or MAS for money safety

Check trading conditions and account types, select the ones suitable for your trading strategy

Find their spreads and commission for fair fees

Reach out to their Customer Support and Education resources for support

BEST FOREX BROKERS 2022

Here I made a selection of Top Forex Brokers by category with some of the best-offered trading conditions and transparent conditions.

BDSwiss – Best Overall Forex Broker 2022

BlackBull Markets – Lowest Spread Forex Broker 2022

FP Markets – Best Forex Broker for Beginners 2022

Pepperstone – Best MT5 Forex Broker 2022

HotForex – Best MT4 Forex Broker 2022

Axiory

FBS

FXCC

ICMarkets

FXTM

SOME QUESTIONS AND ANSWERS

Can I trade the Forex market without a broker?

No, retail traders can't trade Forex directly, since you should be an authorized dealer to trade Forex, as well as operate a quite sufficient amount of funds. Hence, Forex Trading Brokers are the companies that provide retail Forex traders access through their platform to operate Forex Market and trade various markets including Commodity Futures, Indices, Bonds, etc.

Do I need license to trade Forex?

Trading via the Forex Broker you may have access to trading without financial or dealer license. Furthermore, there are hundreds of opportunities with a relatively small investment that allows you to trade Forex, do technical analysis and analyze markets almost instantly.

How do I know if my Forex Broker is regulated?

You can check the license and information through the official brokers' website first, and then confirm a license through the official regulatory website, since unscrupulous brokers may easily fake information and reassure of its license while its not true.

FOREX VERSUS STOCKS

Advantage	Forex	Stocks
24-hour Trading	YES	NO
Commission Free Trading	YES	NO
Instant Execution of Market Orders	YES	NO
Short-Selling without an Uptick	YES	NO

- 24-Hour Market

The Forex market is a seamless 24-hour market. Most brokers are open from Sunday at 2PM EST until Friday at 4PM EST with customer service available 24/7. With the opportunity to trade during the U.S., Asian, and European market hours, you can then create your own trading schedule.

- Commission Free Trading

Most Forex brokers don't charge commission or additional transactions fees to trade currencies online or over the phone. Combined with the tight, consistent, and fully transparent spread, Forex trading costs are lesser than those of any other market. The brokers are compensated for theirs services through the bid/ask prices.

- Instantaneous Execution of Market Orders

Your trades are immediately executed under normal market conditions. You also have price surety on every market order under normal market conditions. What you click on is the price you'll get. You will be able to execute directly off real-time streaming prices (Yeah!). There's no discrepancy between the price displayed on the platform and the execution price to enter your trade. Keep in mind that most brokers only guarantee stop limit, as entry orders are only guaranteed under normal market conditions. Fills are instantaneous most of the time, but under extraordinarily volatile market conditions order execution may experience delays.

- Short-Selling without an Uptick

Unlike the equity market, there is no limitations on short selling in the currency market. Trading opportunities exist in the currency market no matter whether a trader is long or short, or which way the market is moving. Since currency trading always involves the purchasing of one currency and selling of another, there is no structural bias to the market. So you always have impartial access to trade in a rising or falling market.

- No Middlemen

Centralized exchanges provide many upper hand to the trader. However, one of the difficulty with any centralized exchange is the involvement of middlemen. Any party that is in between the trader and the buyer/seller of the security or instrument traded will cost them money. The cost can be either in time or in fees. Spot currency trading does away with the middlemen and allows clients to interact directly with the market-maker responsible for the pricing on a particular currency pair. Forex traders get swift access and cheaper costs.

- Buy/Sell programs do not control the market

How many times have you heard that "fund B" was selling "V" or buying "W"? Word has it that the funds were making profits because it's the end of the financial year or because today is "triple witching day", all as an clarification of why this stock is up or the market in general is down or positive on the session. The stock market is very vulnerable to large fund buying and selling.

In spot trading market, the liquidity of the Forex market makes the likelihood of any bank to control a particular currency very slim. Banks, hedge funds, governments, retail currency conversion houses and large net-worth individuals are just some of the participants in the spot currency markets where the liquidity is unprecedented.

- Analysts and brokerage firms are not likely to influence the market.

Have you watched TV lately? Heard about a particular internet stock and an analyst of a reputable brokerage firm accused of keeping its recommendations, such as "buy" when the stock was rapidly declining? It is the nature of these relationships. No matter what the government does to intervene and discourage this type of activity, we have not heard the last of it.

IPO's are big business for both the companies going public and the brokerage houses. Relationships are mutually beneficial and analysts work for the brokerage houses that need the companies as clients. That catch-22 will never disappear.

Foreign exchange, as the prime market, generates billions in revenue for the world's banks and is a necessity of the global markets. Analysts in foreign exchange don't drive the deal flow, they just analyze the Forex market.

PROTECT YOURSELF BEFORE YOU WRECK YOURSELF

Before I move any further, I am going to be 100% honest with you and tell you the following before you can consider trading currencies:

- All Forex traders, and I mean all traders do LOSE money on trades. Ninety percent of traders lose money, significantly due to lack of planning, training and lacking the money management rules. Also, if you don't like to lose or are a super perfectionist, you'll probably have a hard time adjusting to trading.
- Trading Forex is not for the unemployed, people on low incomes, or who can't afford to pay their electricity bill or afford to eat.
- You should have at least a minimum of $10,000 of trading capital (in a mini account) that you can risk to lose. Don't think you can start up a trading account with a few hundred dollars and expect to become a kazillionaire.

The Forex market is one of the most demanded markets for speculation, due to its huge size, liquidity and tendency for currencies to move in strong trends. You would think traders all over the world are making a killing in the business, but sadly success has been limited to very small percentage of traders.

Many traders come to trade with the misguided belief of making a gazillion bucks, but in reality, lack the discipline required for trading. Most people don't even have the discipline to stick to a diet or to go to the gym two to three times a week. If you can't even do that, how do you think you are going to succeed in trading?

Short term trading is **NOT** for amateurs, and it is barely the path to **"GET RICH QUICK"**. You can't make massive profits without taking gigantic risks. A trading strategy that involves taking a high degree of risk means suffering inconsistent trading performance and often suffering huge loss. A trader who does this probably don't have a trading strategy - unless you call **"GAMBLING"** a trading strategy!

Forex Trading is not some **Get-Rich-Quick Schemes!**

Forex Trading is a valuable **SKILL** that takes **TIME** to **LEARN**.

Skilled traders can make money in this field. However, just as we have it in other occupation or career, **SUCCESS** doesn't happen overnight.

Forex trading is not a piece of cake (as some people would want you to believe). Think about it, if it really was, then everyone trading would already be millionaires. The truth is that even some expert traders with years of experience still do encounter periodic losses.

Drill this in your head: that there are **NO** shortcuts to Forex trading. It takes lots and lots of **TIME** to master it.

There is no substitution for hard work and diligence. Practice trading on a **DEMO ACCOUNT** and assume the virtual money is your own real money.

Do **NOT** try to open a live trading account until you are trading **PROFITABLY** on a demo account.

If you can't wait anymore until you're profitable on a demo account, at least try demo trading for 2 months. Hey, at least you were able to withstand losing all your money for two months right? If you can't hold out for the 2 months, cut your hands off trading.

Concentrate on **ONE** major currency pair. It gets far too complicated to keep tabs on more than a currency pair when you've just started trading. Stick with one of the major currencies because they are the most liquid which makes their spreads cheap.

You can be a winner in currency trading, but as in other aspects of life, it will take **HARD-WORK , DEDICATION,** a lot of **COMMON SENSE** , a **LITTLE LUCK** and a whole lot of **GOOD JUDGEMENT.**

TRADING PLATFORMS/INTERFACES

MT 4 AND MT 5

MT 4 stands for Meta trader 4 while MT 5 stands for Meta trader 5.

MetaTrader or MT 4 is an electronic trading platform widely used by online retail foreign exchange speculative traders for trading and analyzing Forex and few other financial markets **WHILE** MetaTrader 5 is the number 1 multi-asset platform preferred by traders and investors from around the globe for trading Forex, CFDs, exchange-traded instruments and futures. The platform proffers advanced charting and trading tools, as well as options for automated trading.

NOTE !!! : MetaTrader 5 is the newest version of the popular MetaTrader platform.

While the MT 5 is newer, it is not really an upgraded version. Both MT 4 and MT 5 are trading platforms with good back-testing capabilities, as well as graphical interfaces that looks exactly similar.

MT 4 and MT 5 are alike in presentation, delivering simple easy-to-use functions on both live and demo accounts. The interface can be downloaded to your desktop computer or mobile phones and then connected with your chosen broker.

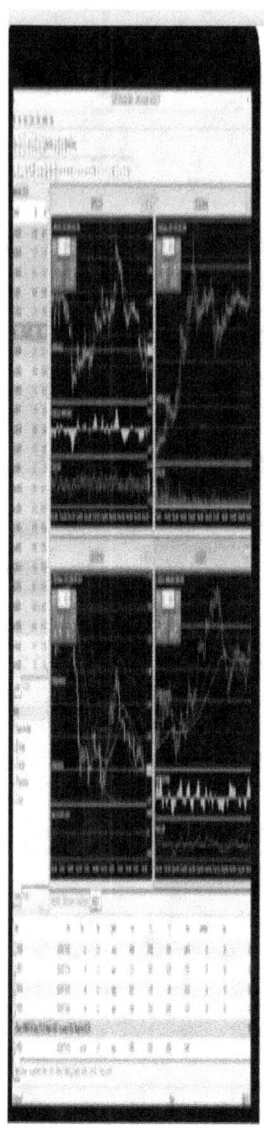

Mt 4 & Mt 5 interface on a computer

Mt 4 symbol on the AppStore

Mt 5 symbol on the AppStore

MONEY MANAGEMENT

This section is one of the most significant sections you will ever read about trading.

Why is it important? Well, we are into the business of making money, and in order to make money we have to learn how to manage it. Ironically, this is one of the most overlooked areas in trading. Many traders are just so anxious to get right into trading with no regards to their total account size. They simply determine how much they can stomach to lose in a single trade and hit the "trade" button. There's a common term for this type of investing….it's called **GAMBLING!**

When you trade the market without money management rules, you are in fact gambling. You are not looking at the long term return on your investment. Instead you are only looking for that "**JACKPOT**". Money management rules will not only guide us, but they will make us very profitable in the long run. If you don't believe me, and you think that "gambling" is the way to get rich, then consider this example:

People go to Las Vegas all the time to gamble their money in hopes to win it big in a jackpot, and in fact many people actually do win. So how on earth, are casino's still making money if many individuals are winning from jackpots? The answer isn't far fetched that while even though people win jackpots in the long run, casino's are still profitable and gaining because they rake in more money from the people that don't win. That is where the word "the house always wins" comes from.

The plain truth here is that casinos are just very rich statisticians. They know that in the long run, they will be the ones making the money—not the gamblers. Even if Joe Schmoe wins $100,000 jackpot in a slot machine, the casinos know that there will be 100 more gamblers who **WON'T** win that jackpot and the money will go right back into their pockets.

This is a basic example of how statisticians make money over gamblers. Even though both lose money, the statistician, or casino in this case study, knows how to control their losses. Indispensable, this is how money management works.If you learn how to control your losses, you will have an high chance at being profitable.

You want to be the rich statistician and **NOT** the gambler because in the long run, you want to "always be the winner."

So how do you become this rich statistician instead of a loser?

Drawdown and Maximum Drawdown?

So we do know nowadays that money management will make us money in the long run, but now I'd like to show you the other side of things. What would really happen if you don't use the money management rules?

Now let's consider this case study. Let's say you have a $100,000 and you lose $50,000. What percentage of your account have you lost? The answer is 50%. Simple enough. Now, what percentage of that $50,000 do you have to make in order to get back to your original $100,000? It's not 50%—you'd have to make back 100% of your $50,000 to get back to your original $100,000. This is called drawdown. For this example, we would've had a 50% drawdown.

The point of that little explanation is that it is very easy to lose money and a lot harder to make it back. I know you're saying to yourself, " I'm not going to lose 50% of my account in one trade." Well I would certainly hope not!

However, what if you lost 3, 5, or even 10 trades in a row? That couldn't possibly happen to you, right? (Sarcasm used) You have a trading system that wins 70% of the time, so there is **NO** way you could lose 10 trades in a row. (Even more sarcasm used)

Well, while you may have a good system, consider this also:

In trading, we are always looking for an edge. That is the whole reason why traders develop systems. A trading system that is 70% profitable sounds like a very good edge to have. But just because your trading system is 70% profitable, doesn't mean for every 100 trades you make, you will win 7 out of every 10. Does it?

Not necessarily! How do you know which 70 out of those 100 trades will be winners?

The answer is that you don't. You could lose the first 30 trades in a row and win the remaining 70. That would still give you a 70% profitable system, but you have to ask yourself, "Would you still be in the game if you lost 30 trades in a row?"

This is why money management is so vital. No matter what system you make use of, you will eventually have a losing streak. Even the professional poker players who make their living through poker go through horrible losing streaks, and yet they still end up profitable.

The real reason is that the good poker players practice money management because they know that they will not win every tournament they play. Instead, they only risk a small percentage of their total bankroll so that they can survive those losing streaks.

This is what you must do as a trader. Only risk a small percentage of your "**trading streak**"so that you can survive your losing streaks. Remember that if you practice strict money management rules, you will become the casino and in the long run, "you will always win."

Let me give you an illustration to what happens when you use proper money management and when you don't.

Don't Lose Your Shirt

Here is a short illustration that will show you the contrast between risking a small percentage of your capital compared to risking a higher percentage.

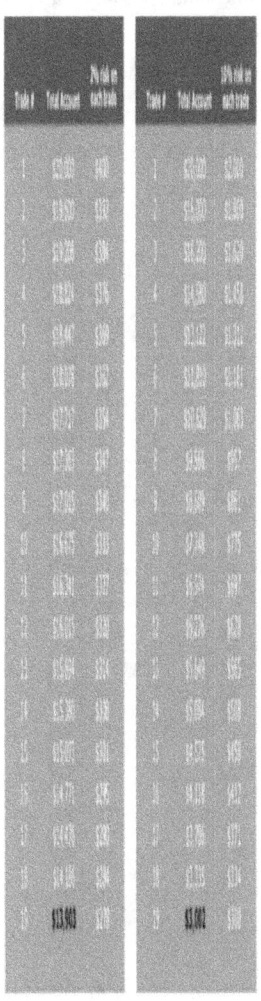

You can see that there is a big difference between risking 2% of your account compared to risking 10% of your account on a single trade. If you happened to go through a losing streak and lost only 19 trades in a row, you would've went from starting with $20,000 to having only $3,002 left if you risked 10% on each trade. You would've lost over 85% of your account! If you risked only 2% you would've still had $13,903 which is only a 30% loss of your total account.

Of course, the last thing I want to do is lose 19 trades in a row, but even if you only lost 5 trades in a row, look at the difference between risking 2% and 10%. If you risked 2% you would still have $18,447. If you risked 10% you would only have $13,122. That's less than what you would've had even if you lost all 19 trades and risked only 2% of your account!

The point of this illustration is that you want to setup your money management rules so that when you do have a drawdown period (losing streak) you will still have enough capital to stay in the game. Can you imagine if you lost 85% of your account? You would have to make 566% on what you are left with in order to get back to breakeven. Trust me, you do **NOT** want to be in that position. In fact, here is a chart that will illustrate what percentage you would have to make to breakeven if you were to lose a certain percentage of your account.

Loss of Capital	% required to get back to breakeven
10%	11%
20%	25%
30%	43%
40%	67%
50%	100%
60%	150%
70%	233%
80%	400%
90%	900%

You can see that the more you lose, the harder it is to make it back to your original account size. This is all the more reason that you should do everything you can to protect your account.

So by now, I hope you have gotten it drilled in your head that you should only risk a small percentage of your account in each trade so that you can survive your losing streaks and also to avoid a large drawdown in your account. Remember, you want to be the casino…**NOT** the gambler!

Risk to Reward

Another way you can increase your chances of profitability is to trade when you have the potential to make 3 times more than you are risking. If you give yourself a 3:1 reward/risk ratio, you have a significantly greater chance of ending up profitable in the long run. Take a look at this chart as an example:

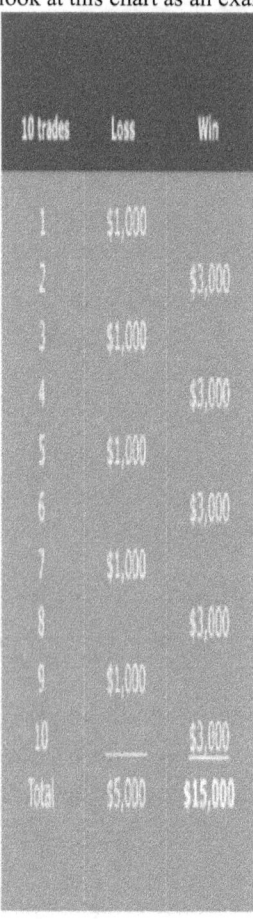

10 trades	Loss	Win
1	$1,000	
2		$3,000
3	$1,000	
4		$3,000
5	$1,000	
6		$3,000
7	$1,000	
8		$3,000
9	$1,000	
10		$3,000
Total	$5,000	$15,000

In this sample above, you can see that even if you only won 50% of your trades, you would still make a profit of $10,000. Just remember that whenever you trade with a good risk to reward ratio, your chances of being profitable are much greater even if you have a lower win percentage.

Summary

Be the casino, not the gambler! Remember, casinos are just very rich statisticians!

Draw down is a reality and **WILL** happen to you at some point. The less you risk in a trade, the less your maximum draw down will be.

The more you lose in your account, the harder it is to make it back to break even.

Trade only a small percentage of your account. The smaller the better. 3% or less is recommended.

It is advisable to trade when you have a high risk to reward ratio. The higher the ratio, the less you have to be right.

WHY HAVE A TRADING PLAN?

Uh oh! You've learned so much and have come so far in your knowledge about Forex, and yet you're still don't have anything to show for. No, you aren't dumb, **BUT** you didn't have a trading plan.

My point is that you can fill your mind with lot of information, but without a good trading plan and the discipline to abide by it, you will **NEVER** be profitable.

Think of your trading plan as your map or guideline to success. It will be a continual reminder of how you will make money in this market. Of course it's not required, and if you can make your living by trading without a plan, I will bow down and hail you as the Market Zeus of the Forex.

So you **CAN** actually trade without a plan if you want, but before you make that decision, let me give you a few reasons **WHY** you should have one.

Why Have a Trading Plan?

Reason 1: It will keep you in the right direction

Consistency is very vital to have in your trading routine because it allows you to truly know how successful you are as a trader. If you have a good trading system but always break your rules, how can you ever really know how good your system really is? Your trading plan will keep you on the track. Read it every day and stick with it.

Reason 2: Trading is a business and successful and productive businesses **ALWAYS** have plans.

I have never seen a successful business that does not start out with a plan. Do you really think Walmart was just created on a whim and then magically became successful? Or what about McDonalds? I'm pretty sure almost anyone can make a better hamburger than McDonalds, but the difference between them and the individual is that they have a successful business plan that guides them to success.

In the same way, you can be able to relate the McDonald's story to your trading career. Whether it be luck or experience, everyone can make money in the Forex. However, the big difference between a losing trader and a successful trader is the **PLAN**. If you have a good trading plan and you are disciplined enough to abide by it, you will be successful!

Now you understand why you should have a trading plan. Let's take a look at what makes up a trading plan.

What Should be in Your Trading Plan?

Trading plans can be as simple or complex as you want it to be, but the most important thing is that you actually **HAVE** a plan and you **FOLLOW** the plan. With that said, here are some of the basic things that every trading plan should have.

1. A trading system

This is the heart of your trading plan. This system should be one that you have thoroughly tested, and have traded for at least two months on a demo account.

Add all the necessary information about your system such as: time frames you use, point for entries and exits, how much you risk during each trade, which currency pair(s) you trade and how many lots you trade.

Example: I'm an intra-day trader and I trade off of the 10 minute charts. I enter a trade when there is a moving average crossover and all my indicators support the direction. I only trade the EUR/USD and I risk no more than 2% of my account on each trade. For now, I trade 5 mini lots and will increase my lot size according to my 2% money management rules.

2. Your trading routine

This is a vital part of your plan because it will ascertain three very important things: when you will analyze the market and plan your trades, when you will actually look at the market to take trades, and when you will evaluate your actions during your trading day.

3. Your mindset

Make enquiries from any trader out there and they will all tell you that one of the hardest things to do when trading is to take out your emotions from it. This segment of your trading plan will depict what frame of mind you will be in when you are trading.

Example: I will see what is on the charts and not what I feel like seeing. No matter how biased I am towards a direction, I will make sure to trade only what my eyes see and not what my feelings tell me. I will not take "**REVENGE**" on the market if I lose on a trade. I will not blame myself if I make a losing trade. Instead I will take it as a learning experience and continue.

4. Your weaknesses

Yes, we all have our weaknesses. We just don't like talking about them. But query yourself this, "How will you ever get better, if you don't own up to what you need to work on?" This section will be an objective way to keep track of things that you need to work on in order to become a better trader.

Example: I tend to over trade. Whenever I lose on a position, I get upset and immediately try to get "**REVENGE**" on the market. I tend to exit early on trades. I don't follow the rules of my system every time I don't comply with my money management rules every time

5. Your goals

"To make a lot of money" is actually not a good goal. Sit down and really think about what you want to achieve as a trader. Do you really want to trade for a living? How much profit can you realistically expect from trading based on your knowledge and experience? Your goals don't even have to be all about making money. These goals can be personal. What do YOU hope to get from this? Use these goals as an encouragement when times get rough. These goals should be your vision, and you must always keep your eyes on the prize!

6. Your trading journal

This will be a priceless tool to helping you become a better trader. Make sure you note all your trades and why you took them. Later down the road you can take a look back and evaluate all your trades and see how you are progressing. I've looked back at my trade journal and have seen just how much I've progressed as a trader. My first entries were very basic and as I've progressed, my trades now make more sense to me now. I've gained a lot of confidence throughout my career and by looking back at my trades, I've really been able to assess myself and see if I am getting closer to my goals. This tool will help you a lot in the long run, so take a few minutes each day and log your trades. You'll be happy you did!

Summary

Your trading plan acts as your trading "**BIBLE**".

Read it everyday and stick to it. You may have all the trading tools in the world, but if you don't have a plan on how you will use them, you can never be successful.

Remember, you are starting a business, and if you want your business to work out, you need to have a **PLAN!**

ARE YOU WILLING TO PAY THE PRICE?

If you really thought that there are actually some ways for a lazy Forex trader to get rich, **SHAME ON YOU!**

No such thing exists. The words "lazy" and "trader" is an oxymoron. You have to be ready to pay the price to become a trader. Which brings about our next lesson.

So, you've gone through the Beginner's guide to Forex trading…five times, learned money management techniques, and maybe even opened up a demo account and started trading a plan you've created. (You do have a trading plan right?) Now you think you can sit back and relax because it's easy money from here on out, right?— **Wrong!**

You've just taken the first step. You've only gotten familiarized with the very basic fundamentals of what it takes to become a professional trader. Now it's the time to get on to the real work.

I'm pretty sure you're now thinking, "There's more to learn?!" Well, mate, the learning never ends.

As it is with any profession, whether you're a doctor, lawyer, athlete, assassin, spy, ninja, ultimate fighter, musician or any other occupation that requires a high level of skill, you can never stop learning and practicing. Else, your skills will deteriorate and you'll slowly forget what you've learned.

This lesson will give you a glance into what it takes – **Education, Time, Money and Psychological stamina** – to get into the most financially rewarding career on the planet: a professional trader.

Education

Just picture yourself in a legal situation and you decide to hire the cheapest lawyer you could find. On the very day you have to stand in front of a jury, then your lawyer says to you, "Don't worry, though this is my first time, I've read 'How to be an Awesome Lawyer in 30 Days for Idiots' a couple of times, so I know what I'm doing. You'll be fine."

Do you think your investment in such lawyer will pay off? Probably not.

You are probably going to end up in the prison with a tattoo covered cellmate named "Killer" for the rest of your life.

Now I'm not a professional lawyer of some sort, but I'm pretty sure and know that it takes more than a book to become one. More likely, lawyers have read and studied a wide range of books, journals and case studies and so on in order to fine-tune their practice. So why would it be any different in becoming a professional trader?

Trading involves becoming skilled in many disciplines including fundamental analysis, technical analysis, sentiment analysis and self-awareness (also known as trading psychology or what I call "mental analysis").

In those disciplines are so many different topics that should be studied individually.

If you shorten your education to a basic high-level overview of a few subjects, how do you think that will help you gain the skills needed to become a successful trader?

I'm not saying you should go out there and read everything there is to read on trading. While that could be ideal, realistically it's not possible.

What I am putting up with is this...

Before you go into a single trade, read and study enough to know why a tool works, how it works and how well it has worked in so many different situations. After you could have start trading your live account, continue reading and studying some more. The Forex market is so dynamic and it is continuously changing. (What market isn't?) Being versatile in all the disciplines of trading gives you the ability to adapt and make quick decisions in this fast-paced market.

Time

Have you ever told yourself there's never enough time in a day? I think we've all thought that to ourselves at some point, but if you're not ready to shift your priorities to make time for trading, then forget about becoming a trader.

Sorry to put this so bluntly, but contrary to popular belief, trading is not some hobbies. Trading is not a hobby.

Trading is not a hobby unless you want to lose your money.

Golf is my hobby. I pay to play golf. Golf is Tiger Wood's business. Tiger Woods are paid to play golf.

Note the difference? Trading is a business. You have to devote yourself to trading just like you would with any other business in order to be successful in it.

So, it's time (pun intended though) to ask yourself this: "Can I balance my time and adjust my lifestyle to give room for trading?"

I'd love to hear a resounding "**YES!**" But before you can actually give an answer to that question, you need to first figure out what your daily priorities are and determine whether or not you can make trading **THE** number **ONE** priority.

A good way to find this out for yourself is to make a list of your daily activities, and then prioritize them. If your daily priorities take up all of your time, then overlook trading as a thing for you.

So, take your time to figure out what is going on in your life because it's very important to balance your time and priorities, not just to becoming a successful trader, but also to live a content and meaningful life. We all want to be extremely profitable, and initially we may drop everything else to get there, but at the end an unbalanced life may lead to a personal and/or professional failure.

Capital aka Cash/Money

It takes money to make money. We all know that, but how much is required to get started in trading? The response actually depends totally on your approach to your new start-up business.

First, take into consideration how you are going to be educated. There are many diverse ways in learning how to trade: Be it from classes, having mentors, on your own, or any combination of the three.

Even though there are many classes and mentors out there willing to teach Forex trading, most will likely charge a fee. The advantage of this route is that a well-taught class or a great mentor can greatly shorten your learning curve and get you on your way to profitability in a much more shorter period of time compared to doing everything yourself.

The drawback is the upfront cost for these programs, which can range from a few hundred to a few thousand dollars, depending on which program you decide to go for. For many of those who are new to trading, the money required to purchase these programs are not available.

For those of you unable to raise up the cash for education, the great news is that most of the information you need to get started can be found for FREE on the internet through brokers, articles and websites.

This is no one "**CORRECT**" path. As long as you are disciplined and also focused on learning the markets, your chances of success increase tremendously. You'll have to be a gung ho student. If not, you may end up in the poor house.

Second, is your manner of approach to the markets going to require special tools such as news feeds or charting software? As a technical trader, most of the charting packages that comes with your broker's trading platform are enough (and some are actually quite good). For those who need special indicators for better functionality, higher end charting software can start at around $100 per month. Probably you're a fundamental trader and you need the news the millisecond it is released, or even before it happens (wouldn't that be nice!). Well, an eye blink and accurate news feeds run from a few hundred to a few thousand dollars per month. Also, you can get a complimentary news feed from your broker, but for some, that extra second or two can be the unlikeness between a profitable or unprofitable trade.

Finally, you'll need some capital to trade. How much exactly? Well, to be honest here. If you're consistent and exercise proper money management techniques, and without even knowing your monthly expenses, then you can probably begin with $50k to $100k in trading capital. It's common knowledge that most of businesses fail due to undercapitalization, which is exactly true in the Forex trading business. Even though you are not able to start with a large amount that you can afford to lose, be patient, save up and learn to trade the right way until you are financially ready.

Psychology

Once you've created the time to get properly educated, do demo trade, and save up sufficient capital, the time will come where you will have to tackle the markets. By this time you should've have be knowledgeable about the mechanics of trading and methods to analyze the market that you are most confident using.

But are you really willing to risk your hard-earned money? Can you put your cash where your mouth is? Can you put up with the (emotional, psychological and financial/economic) pressure of the occasional losing streak and account draw down?

Will you be able to control your enthusiasm on a profitable trade? Can you forget your last trade and completely focus on your next opportunity?

What differentiates the profitable traders from the unprofitable ones is that profitable traders can handle the pressure of risk and control their emotions. They do realize that losing is just a part of business. Those who have enough assurance in their methods and systems know that a draw back is a short-term setback and they will soon recover.

This final crucial lesson can't really be taught. It will take time and experience. You have to put in the hours. You will have to pass through a gazillion different trades and different market environments before you grasp and live these concepts. If you can't do this or aren't willing or ready to, then unfortunately, trading may not be for you.

Summary

For those ready to take the challenge and follow through, professional trading can be a worthwhile goal. But before you can go too deep into Forex trading, dip your toe or get your feet wet in the shallow end first, and become familiar with the water. As you are getting more comfortable, make your way slowly to the deeper end. Take your time.

- Be honest with yourself.
- Be ready and willing to sacrifice your time and money.
- Never stop learning and, most importantly,
- Never quit.

Winners don't and never quit while quitters never win. The cost of becoming top trader is extremely high, but certainly worth it.

FOREX SCAMS

Don't be a sucker.

The first things you must learn about the Forex market is that though it may be enjoyable and exciting, there is no magic button that will instantly turn your pennies into millions of dollars. You may have already come across Forex scams that are filling the marketplace. These companies purposely mislead people into thinking that making money in the Forex is so easy and that they have the "Magic Solution" to raking in booku bucks with a simple click of a button.

Sadly, the number of Forex scams is rising. The Commodities Futures Trading Commission (CFTC) released a report stating that in recent years, they have seen a sharp increase in the rise of Foreign Exchange scams. The CFTC alerts consumers to be careful of sales solicitations on the internet. You might have probably seen some of these companies. I do hear about them all the time from people whenever I try to explain about the Forex market to them. The first thing they say is that they think the Forex is a scam which is absurd. That really makes me so furious! Forex is a massive investment opportunity for people and because of these scammers, they tend to miss out on a good way to make money.

The truth is that no matter how we analyze it, education is the only fool proof way to continually make money in the Foreign Exchange. Even after you finish reading through this book, your journey as a FX trader is only the beginning. I have never seen a successful Forex trader who stopped learning. There is always something new to learn and you must continue to seek out as much information as you can.

The best of your investment you can ever make is in yourself.

Don't spend your money on a company that promises huge returns; even if they show you their track records. It may look pretty and colorful; and I'm sure that the line on the graph that seems to keep going higher makes it look like there is no way you could lose money, but don't let them deceive you. In fact, I could take my broker statement instantly, touch it up with Photo shop and voila! – I have just become the most successful trader on the planet. Pretty impressive huh? I know I'm laying it on pretty thick, but I just want to prevent you from falling into any traps. Instead of giving out your hard earned money to someone else, you could put that money aside into a trading account and take the time to educate yourself.

Note that I didn't say you should put your money into a trading account and start trading.

Save that money in your account and gradually add to it as you continue to learn. Before you realize, your account size will be bigger than you. And to top it off, you'll have a lot of Forex education under your "traders" belt.

So remember, Forex scams **DO** exist. Beware of them and hold onto your money. The great news is that there **ARE** legitimate Forex companies out there. Make sure you do an intensive research on a company if you are thinking about giving them a shot. There is a lot of information on the Internet so do your thing and you'll just be fine.

www.ingramcontent.com/pod-product-compliance
Lightning Source LLC
Chambersburg PA
CBHW071147240526
45465CB00024BA/1811